KU-770-704

Prehistory
of the
Somerset Levels

by

J. M. Coles

and

B. J. Orme

Somerset Levels Project, 1982

The Somerset Levels are an area unique in the British Isles. The region consists of low-lying peat moors interrupted by numerous islands of sand and rock, and it is bordered by the Mendip and Quantock Hills. This uneven landscape was occupied and intensively exploited by prehistoric man for over 4000 years, up to the time of the Roman Conquest. The area is unique for archaeology because it still contains a vast array of evidence about the past, buried deep within the peats. Most of this evidence consists of wood, but there are other objects as well, of pottery, stone, flint and bronze. These provide a graphic picture of man's activities in the Levels, and they can be combined with environmental evidence, from pollen, beetles, and other studies, to give us a detailed picture, or set of pictures, of early man in his landscape.

This book provides an up-to-date guide to the evidence recovered by archaeology in the past 100 years, including the excavations of the Lake Villages carried out by A. Bulleid and H. St. George Gray at the turn of the century, and the most recent results of combined fieldwork, excavation and environmental studies. The first section of the book deals with the discovery and retrieval of the evidence, through commercial peat-cutting and through planned archaeological work. It also examines the various ways in which the evidence is studied, using pollen analysis and experimental reconstruction as well as more traditional archaeological approaches. The second section presents the results of these investigations within a chronological framework.

The story of man in the Levels goes back several thousand years to a time when the area consisted of a vast inlet of the sea with many small islands of sand and rock providing refuge and campsites for hunters and gatherers who occasionally visited the area. They possessed dugouts or rafts which allowed them to move across the watery landscape between the hills and islands, and they pursued a shadowy existence until the arrival of the first farmers c. 6000 years ago. These farmers, newly arrived in Britain with their knowledge of cereal cultivation and perhaps the domestication of animals such as sheep and cattle, settled the barely-touched lands and began to clear the dense forests in many areas, selecting the best land for their crops and pastures. Because agriculture does not yield an 'instant' food supply, they often chose areas such as the Somerset Levels where they could work the land and also hunt, fish and gather wild foods from the hills and the marshlands. The prehistory of the Levels from 4000 B.C. until the Roman occupation is remarkable in that we can see a constant presence of man in the area, always working the land, using the forests, the meadows, the islands and the watery marshes in the need to produce food and provide shelter for his family. Although conditions changed quite remarkably through the 4000 years of prehistoric occupation, these basic needs could always be achieved, or so it seems according to the archaeological evidence.

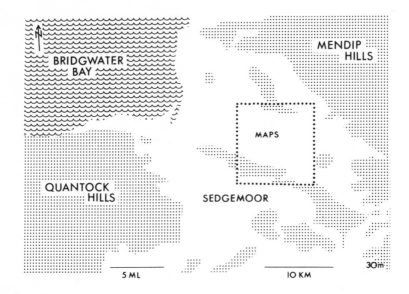

Great reed swamps began to form around 4500 B.C., at first with brackish waters, then with fresh water which encouraged the growth of the *Phragmites* reed, standing up to 3m (10 feet) tall. Subsequently, the growth of peat and the development of a fen woodland over much of the area marked a drying of the landscape and created better conditions for farmers and herdsmen; many platforms and trackways across the irregular and uneven landscape mark their presence, and their need to move between farmsteads and fields and wild lands. Later still, from about 3000 B.C. an increase in rainfall created severe floodwater conditions in places, drowned the fen woodland and caused the growth of raised bog which must have posed severe problems for both farmers and herdsmen. Yet eventually they seem to have achieved a 'working relationship' with the great raised bog of the Levels, both north and south of the Polden Hills. Farming continued, but now perhaps with more emphasis on the herding of cattle, the pannage of pigs in the woodlands of the hills, and the hand-digging of plots of ground for vegetables on the slopes of the hills. Seasonal flooding of the marshes would have encouraged fishing, fowling and the gathering of wild plants, and the summer drying of the lands would have created ideal grazing conditions for cattle on the meadowlands around the edges of the great Levels. These conditions persisted into historic times, and indeed still influence farming practices today.

The prehistoric story of the Levels has been revealed mainly in the valley of the Brue, north of the Polden Hills, but there is evidence that ancient man was also present in Sedgemoor, south of the Poldens. Little archaeological work has been completed on Sedgemoor, and so we have concentrated our attention on the northern part of the Levels.

This survey is of a period without written evidence. The reader will find both an outline of the prehistory of one small region of the British Isles, and a demonstration of how much of our remote past can now be recovered by the archaeologist, and how much still remains to be discovered and understood.

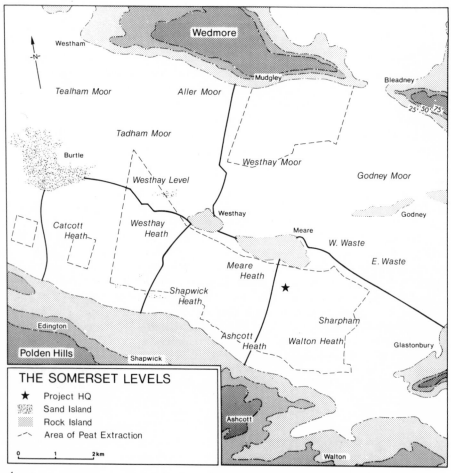

THE SOMERSET LEVELS

★   Project HQ
   Sand Island
   Rock Island
   Area of Peat Extraction

0   1   2km

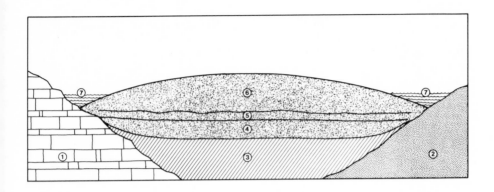

LOCAL GEOLOGY AND PEAT GROWTH

Around 10,000 years ago, the icesheets of the northern hemisphere began to melt, the sea level rose, and many coastal areas became flooded. Among these was the broad valley system which drained the land between the Mendips and the Quantocks into the Bristol Channel. For several thousand years this low-lying area was under sea-water, the surface broken only by the narrow limestone ridge of the Poldens(1) and occasional small islands of rock or sand(2). The drowned valley floor was gradually blanketed in silt and clays(3) laid down by the seawaters and interleaved with thin lenses of peat, formed during temporary lowerings of the sea level.

Towards 4500 B.C., the sea retreated from the Levels, leaving behind a swampy estuarine area soon colonised by reeds. The dominant species was *Phragmites* (Norfolk reed) which flourished in the deep brackish waters and in the succeeding freshwater marsh. As the plants died, they fell into the water and sank below the surface, where decay was arrested due to the absence of oxygen, bacteria and fungi. With time, the mat of dead plants grew thicker and thicker, forming a first layer of peat(4) over the marine clay. More varied marsh plants were now able to colonise the area, including bogbeans and several species of moss and sedges. One of the sedges, *Cladium*, flourishes where there is water up to 40 cm deep, and its presence in the plant community during this time indicates a very wet environment enriched by calcareous water off the limestone hills.

The continuous accumulation of peat gradually raised the ground surface above water level, perhaps only in a few places for a few summer months at first, but enough for water-tolerant trees such as birch and alder to colonise small patches amidst the reed swamp. Gradually, these patches extended as the trees contributed their own dead leaves and branches and root systems to the ever-growing peat. By 3500 B.C., fenwood(5) had replaced much of the reed swamp vegetation. The birch, willow and alder thickets were interspersed with more open areas of moss and sedge and some remaining reed pools.

5

The fenwood in turn yielded to species typical of a raised bog(6): sphagnum moss, cottongrass and heather. These plants prefer acid to calcareous conditions and they indicate that the Levels were poorly drained and lacking in mineral nourishment. Rainfall was the major source of water. The run-off from the limestone hills flowed away along the base of the slopes, in a lagg(7) where trees still grew, but otherwise the rather bleak expanse of moorland was broken only here and there by stagnant pools of water, clumps of shrubby plants like bog myrtle, and the occasional tree. Flooding of the Levels occurred from time to time, for relatively short intervals, and the raised bog environment persisted until about 400 A.D. when peat growth ceased.

Originally, the river Brue skirted Glastonbury Tor, flowed along the eastern edge of the Levels and north through the Bleadney Gap. Drainage was otherwise very poor, with winter flooding the norm, and many efforts were made by the mediaeval inhabitants of the region to improve matters. The most extensive operations were those of the Glastonbury monks, who diverted the Brue into an artificial channel running due west through the Levels. Their efforts may well have created the vast Meare Pool, a shallow lake full of fish and wild fowl that contributed significantly to the **mediaeval economy of the Levels.**

Peat-cutting

The growth of the great raised bogs of the Somerset Levels resulted in very thick accumulations of peat, many metres thick in places. This peat is often dark, humified and rich, and it has been a source of fuel, fertiliser and building blocks for many centuries. Cutting may have begun in the Romano-British period, and by mediaeval times valuable rights to cut peat were established over much of the Levels. Until very recently, the blocks of peat, called mumps, were cut out by hand using a peat-saw and spades; after drying, they were turned and stacked into beehive-shaped ruckles which still dominate the peat fields today.

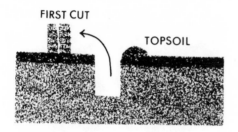

FIRST CUT

TOPSOIL

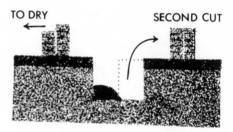

TO DRY

SECOND CUT

   Machines have now replaced the hand-cutters, and the predominant use for the peat has changed from fuel to fertiliser. Machine-cutting requires careful planning over several years. First, the area to be cut must be drained, always a difficult operation in the very flat environment of the Levels, but it is said that the experts are now so skilled they can persuade the water to flow away uphill! Be that as it may, once the water table has been lowered, the field is marked out in trenches to be cut and the vegetation and topsoil removed by scraping-machines, an operation known as unridding. A cutting machine is then set to move slowly down the line of a trench, or head, cutting out blocks of peat as it goes and stacking them neatly on the surface beside the trench. When the blocks are partly dried, they are turned and then stacked in ruckles until the peat is well-dried. It is then transported to the peat factory where it is processed and packed in the familiar polythene bags which are to be seen on sale across the country.
   A comparison of the rates of extraction by hand-cutting and by machine will show what a difference the introduction of the machines has made to the peat industry of the Levels. Although an expert hand-cutter can extract many mumps of peat per day, a machine has an output 15 times as great and the most recent methods of cutting, by rotovation and block cutting, are even more rapid.

ARCHAEOLOGY

The gradual accumulation of peat in the Levels engulfed and preserved a quantity of evidence about the activities of prehistoric man. Peat-cutting exposes the evidence anew, from two to six thousand years later. Part of this evidence consists of substantial wooden trackways, and these have long been recognised as the artifacts of early man. In the later 19th century, two local antiquaries began fieldwork in the Levels. C. W. Dymond recorded the Abbot's Way (p. 40), and Arthur Bulleid began a search for sites similar to the well-known prehistoric Swiss Lake Villages. He was rewarded by the discovery of Iron Age settlements at Godney near Glastonbury (p. 52), and at Meare, and in later years made many finds of stray objects and trackways. This work was continued by Stephen Dewar, who worked with Harry Godwin, then pioneering palaeo-environmental investigations; together they began a fruitful partnership of archaeological and botanical fieldwork aimed at reconstructing past environments and their effect on early man.

As the rate of peat-cutting expanded, more and more fieldwork was required to keep abreast of the archaeological finds exposed by the cutting. The Department of Archaeology at Cambridge University organised a series of excavations, and in 1973 the Somerset Levels Project was established with financial support from the Department of the Environment and other bodies. Since that date, a full-time Field Archaeologist has been based in the Levels.

The Field Archaeologist works in a number of ways, much influenced by the time of year and variations in the rate of peat-cutting. The most important task is to walk every single head of all the peat-cutting fields, searching the sections and the mumps for archaeological evidence. The most common type of find is worked wood, sometimes a single slight pole with an axed end — perhaps a spear lost by a hunter? — and sometimes a mass of branches macerated in the blades of a machine which trundled through a brushwood-bundle trackway.

But one person cannot see everything, and many finds are still due to peat-cutters, people who turn and stack the peat for drying, farmers clearing their ditches, and the other people at work on the moors and in the surrounding fields. One machine driver found a flint axe, which the blades of his machine missed by millimetres. Another, unridding with a hymac, revealed a trackway made of hurdles. One cutter, clearing out a ditch by hand, found worked wood which we now know to belong to the oldest wooden trackway in Europe, the Sweet Track. The Field Archaeologist is in contact with all the people who might make such finds, regularly talking to all the peat-workers and to farmers, sometimes talking to local schools and other groups, and sometimes calling in at the best of local information centres, the pub.

Excavation

Over the course of a year, a number of finds are made in the Levels and some of them belong to apparently large features or structures, which lie in areas of future peat extraction. The archaeologists of the Project select from these the features which look potentially most interesting, and reserve the area around them for excavation. Excavations take place at all times of year, with large sites tackled in the summer when a full team of volunteers, supervisors, environmental specialists and directors can be assembled. People from as far afield as Finland, Poland, Canada, Australia and Japan have worked on excavations in the Levels and the majority of volunteers are students. With the site chosen and a team assembled, the excavation can begin, often (thanks to the peat companies) with the aid of a machine that scrapes away any overburden of peat. This help is very welcome, as the feature to be investigated may lie a metre or more below the ground surface. Meanwhile, the digging equipment is brought to the site: planks, wooden boxes and toe-boards for keeping people off the soft peat surface, spades and plastic spatulae for digging the peat and buckets to remove it in, watering cans, tanks and quantities of polythene to keep the wood wet once it is exposed, and sometimes a tent to keep the diggers dry at lunchtime.

Machining stops well clear of the prehistoric structure, and the workers take over with spades, gently loosening small lumps of peat for removal. As soon as wood appears, spades are abandoned for small plastic **spatulae**, and the workers squat on short boards along the edge of the site, scraping away thin layers of peat so that the ancient wooden remains are just visible.

Because the peat and the wood are soft, workers must keep off the site surface. To do this, they are suspended on planks held by boxes on the edges of the site; sometimes work can be carried out by using 'toeboards' placed flat on the surface of the peat, but never on the wood of course.

As the work progresses, more and more wood is revealed, and patience and a steady hand are needed to remove the final flecks of peat with spatulae, icelolly sticks, paint brushes, and fingers.

On sunny days the steam rises off the peat, and even on dull and cold days moisture is lost from the site unless it is raining quite hard. The prehistoric wood may have a 95% water content, and if it is not kept permanently wet it cracks and splits and shrinks. Therefore the site is regularly watered — all the time on hot or sunny days, and every hour or so on a damp winter's dig, and any part which is not being worked on is covered with polythene. At night the whole site is covered with one or more layers of polythene. In this way, it is possible to preserve the wood in a fresh condition for a week, but even with constant attention longer exposure leads to decay, and therefore all the excavations in the Levels are planned so that the wood is fully exposed for the shortest possible time.

When the site is clean, it is recorded. Numerous photographs are taken, from all angles, with close-ups of all the interesting features. The site has to be planned to scale, and this can be done either by drawing or, when speed is required, by taking vertical photographs: for either method a string grid of metre or smaller squares is laid out to assist the planning. If photography is used, the film is developed and printed to scale immediately, and the prints stuck together to form a mosaic of the site that can be used in the same manner as a drawn plan for the next stage of the excavation, the lifting.

The aims of lifting the structure are to discover how it was put together by prehistoric man, to record the lowest pieces, to take many objects for preservation, and to select a great variety of samples for environmental and dating evidence.

Conservation

The conservation of wooden objects from the peats of the Levels poses many problems. The wooden posts, pegs, boards, planks and tools are all heavily water-logged, saturated with water and extremely fragile. Their surface is soft and easily damaged by finger pressure, and often they have to be supported on 'lifting boards', or bandaged completely, before they can be freely moved. Internally, the wood is severely degraded, and much of its cellular structure is destroyed. Not many conservation laboratories exist in Britain, and few have the capacity to take loads of soggy wood from Somerset. Hence a small laboratory has been set up in the middle of the Levels to conserve the wood recovered by the excavations.

The drawings show axe-marks on wooden pegs made about 6000 years ago, and now conserved for future study. The scale, and others in this book, are marked in centimetres.

A variety of conservation methods has been tried, including dehydration and impregnation with rosin, and replacement of water by wax. The wax method is by far the most successful and is the only method now used in the Levels.

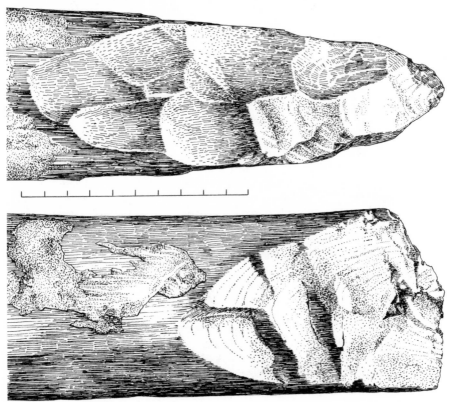

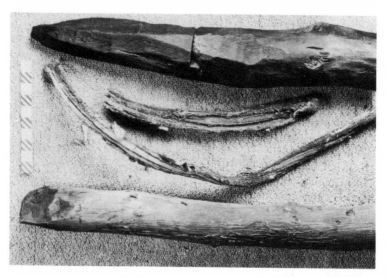

The wood is brought to the laboratory wrapped in foam or bandages, and it is then cleaned in fresh water, measured and photographed from all essential angles. Following this, the wood is firmly bandaged again and tied in position on a metal grid frame which is lowered into one of a series of fibreglass tanks. The tanks contain a solution of one-third wax (a water-soluble wax called Polyethylene Glycol 4000) and two-thirds water.

After about three months cold soak, tank heaters are switched on and the temperature is slowly raised month by month to a maximum of 55 degrees Celsius (131 degrees Fahrenheit). By the time this temperature has been reached, much of the water has evaporated and the volume of liquid in the tank has been maintained at its original level by adding melted wax until the solution is almost 100% wax; it is very hot and must be kept hot as otherwise it would congeal into a huge block of solid wax and the wood would probably be destroyed. During this heating process, the water in the wood is drawn out into the general tank liquid and is replaced by the water-wax solution, and eventually by almost 100% wax. When this replacement is complete, a matter of nine months, the wood can be withdrawn from the tank, unbandaged and wiped clean with great care. When the wax hardens, the wooden object is preserved and can be handled freely; it turns rather dark but all of the prehistoric workmanship has survived intact and the piece is ready for display or storage for future studies. The need to conduct this wax process can be vividly seen in the photograph of four pieces of wood, all originally of the same size: the topmost piece is still wet and untreated, the middle pieces were left untreated for a day or two to dry out, and they have severely shrunk and distorted; the lowest piece has been conserved by wax and almost all of the original features can still be seen. Without conservation, the prehistoric wood would only be seen by the **excavator**.

ENVIRONMENTAL STUDIES

Closely associated with the archaeological excavations are a number of environmental studies which help to recreate the landscapes of the prehistoric past. Among these studies, pollen analysis is the most important in terms of the regional environment.

Trees, shrubs, grasses, **weeds** and all other flowering plants release pollen into the air. The minute grains land on exposed surfaces and some eventually become buried, in lake sediments, soils, peat, ditch fills, and the like. Where the pollen grains are incorporated into a peat deposit their chances of survival are good and this is one of the most fruitful sources for environmental studies.

The palaeoenvironmentalist intent on reconstructing the past vegetation of the Levels makes use of this abundant pollen. A monolith is cut out of the peat in sections, with the exact level of each lump carefully recorded, and then taken back to the laboratory where it is subdivided into narrow layers, and broken up to facilitate the removal of the pollen. Different plant species have different-shaped pollen grains, and these can be identified under the microscope. After identifying and counting the grains from each sample, the pollen analyst sorts the species into groups (e.g., tree pollen, grasses, aquatics). From the relative abundance of the different species and groups, he is able to reconstruct in broad terms the plant communities that flourished at the time when the samples accumulated, and to trace the changes in vegetation that took place over the period covered by the monolith.

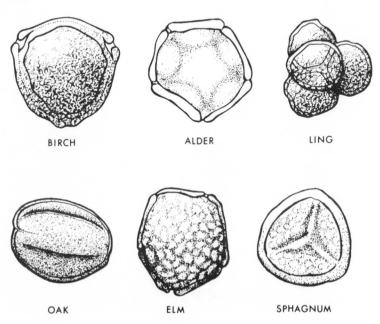

BIRCH   ALDER   LING

OAK   ELM   SPHAGNUM

A typical analysis from the Levels would show the basal layers of a monolith dominated by pollen from trees, with some shrubs and many aquatic plants, reflecting the immediate reed swamp with forest on the drier slopes nearby. These slopes would be cleared by farmers in establishing their fields, and the diagram (eliminating the aquatics to concentrate on other plants) would show a dramatic decline in trees and the rise in plants of open ground, the grasses and herbs for instance. Later on, with abandonment of the fields for one reason or another, the forest would reassert itself and the diagram would show a rise in tree pollen. Radiocarbon dates allow us to detect specific episodes in early agriculture in the Levels, as this diagram from Burtle shows.

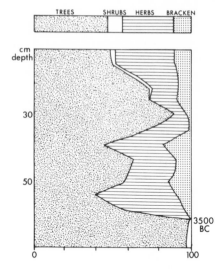

In addition to pollen, recognisable fragments of individual plants may be present in the peat: twig (a), leaf (b), reed (c), seed (d), bits of moss or heather stems. These macroscopic remains can indicate exactly what was growing in the locality, a more precise source of information than the pollen which is blown in from the surrounding region.

18

Beetles

Beetles provide the bulk of animal evidence from the Levels for palaeo-environmental studies. Due to the acidity of the peat, bone and shell decay in most instances, but parts of the exoskeleton of beetles, and fragments of other insects and spiders, may be remarkably well-preserved and can be identified to species level. The picture shows the parts preserved from a water beetle which lived about 3500 years ago in the Levels, compared with a modern example. Some species have very specific habitat requirements, maybe living off a single variety of reed, and the identification of a range of species can provide quite precise information about the local contemporary vegetation and water levels, and occasionally some idea of the local fauna. In general terms, the more varied the species represented, the richer the local environment, whereas a restricted range, such as that identified from the Abbots Way (p. 40), is suggestive of a relatively poor and monotonous plant cover.

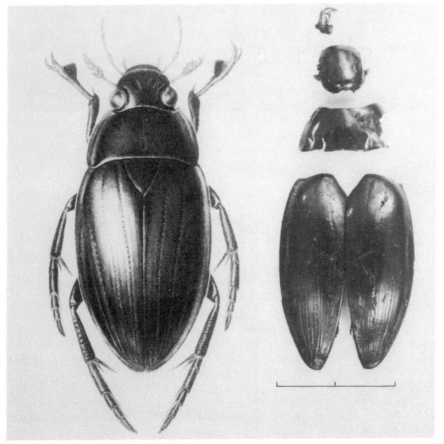

Tree-ring studies

The Somerset Levels are one of the best source areas in the British Isles for prehistoric material suitable for tree-ring studies, thanks to the abundant and well-preserved wood associated with human activity from the Neolithic onwards.

Tree-ring studies begin with well-preserved old oak timbers with many annual growth rings. The widths of these rings vary, depending on the particular climatic conditions, a narrow ring during times of stress through drought for instance, and a wide ring during times of ample nutrients for the tree. Each set of rings tells the story of a tree's life, and if the particular sequence (magnified by use of a logarithmic scale for the ring widths in the illustration) matches that of another piece of

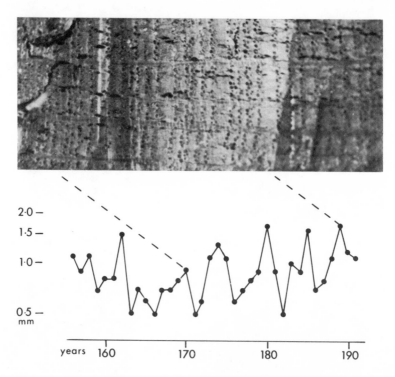

timber, then they are likely to be exactly contemporary. In this way, the various pieces of wood in a trackway or platform can be related to each other. The diagram shows part of an oak plank which has been matched into years 170-190 in a long Neolithic sequence in the Levels.

If timbers are not wholly contemporary, they nonetheless may be related by tree-ring studies if the rings at the edge of one plank match those near the centre of the other; in this way a very long sequence can be built up from many different pieces of wood, extending back many centuries.

COPPICE

POLLARD

Woodland and fungus studies

The examination of the wood from the ancient structures in the peats gives us information about the ways in which man began to use the forests, and to select and control particular trees growing in them. One aspect which archaeology has discovered in the Levels is the abundant evidence for coppicing of woodlands both on the edge of the marshlands and on the drier slopes of the hills and the islands. In coppicing, areas of underwood of hazel or other trees are felled every few years and from the stumps or stools there spring vigorous growths of shoots and poles. These grow several times as fast as uncoppiced saplings, and when harvested, the stool will again be left to produce a new batch of shoots. If cattle or deer are present in the woodlands, the coppiced areas would be fenced, else the tender shoots would be broken or eaten. One way to prevent this is to pollard the trees; this is the same as coppicing except the tree is cut back several metres above the ground, beyond the reach of grazing animals. The Somerset Levels have revealed evidence of coppicing or pollarding from *c.* 4000 B.C. onwards, and this is the earliest sign of woodland management so far recovered anywhere in the world.

Fungus studies are based on the preference of certain fungi for particular habitats. The distinct fruit bodies of the fungi are rarely preserved, but traces may remain of the extensive networks of hyphae in the wood, and occasional distinct zone lines are obvious (as in the photograph), showing the progress of the rot through a piece of wood.

Radiocarbon dating

The technique of radiocarbon dating depends on the presence of carbon in all living matter, whether plant or animal, and the fact that a certain minute but constant proportion of this carbon is radioactive. From the time a plant or an animal dies, the amount of radioactive carbon (^{14}C) steadily declines, relative to the amount of ordinary carbon. The decline, or decay-rate, is known and by measuring the amount of radioactive carbon remaining in organic matter, it is possible to calculate when the original plant or animal died. Wood is an ideal material for providing radiocarbon dates, and peat and charcoal are equally suitable; many dates for the prehistory of the Levels have been obtained from such samples.

Radiocarbon dates are not, however, the equivalent of exact historical dates. The results obtained will be expressed as 3200±80 bc, for example. This means that there is a 68% chance of the date falling in the time span 80 years either side of 3200 (3280 to 3120 bc) and a 98% chance of it falling in twice that time span

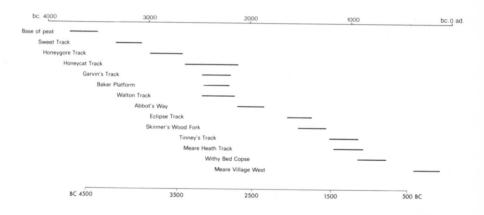

(3360 to 3040 bc). In the first case, the date is said to be given to one standard deviation, and in the second, to two standard deviations. The dates in the chart are all drawn out to two standard deviations.

For reasons which are not yet fully understood, it is apparent that radiocarbon years are not the exact equivalent of calendar years, nor is the degree of variation constant. However, a fairly reliable check can be provided by tree-rings, which can be dated both historically through ring counting and by radiocarbon assay. The results of these two methods are then used together to draw up a calibration chart for the conversion of radiocarbon dates into historical or calendar equivalents. The dates in this booklet have been calibrated using such a chart, and the summary graph shown here depicts radiocarbon years bc along the top, and calendar years B.C. along the bottom.

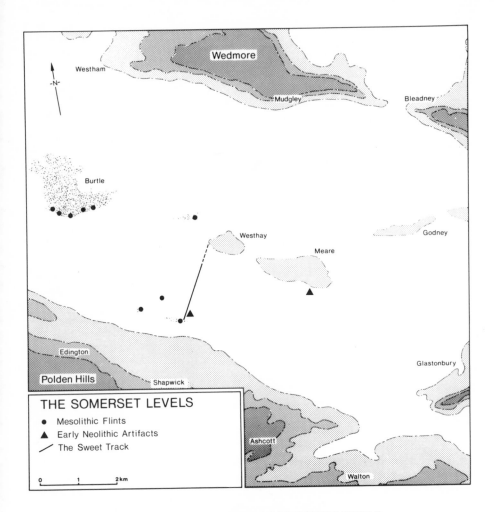

THE SOMERSET LEVELS

● Mesolithic Flints
▲ Early Neolithic Artifacts
╱ The Sweet Track

0   1   2 km

PREHISTORY OF THE SOMERSET LEVELS

The present day peatlands of the Somerset Levels consisted of vast expanses of brackish water in the centuries before 4500 B.C., with a few sand and rock islands projecting above the water and the hill slopes densely wooded. From 4500 B.C. the development of sand dunes to the west prevented tidal flooding of the marshlands by salt waters, and gradually the rivers brought enough inland water into the by-now ponded area to create fresh water conditions. The Levels turned into a huge swamp, with tall reeds disguising the still and deep waters of the great expanses between the hills. The first occupants of the area arrived when this transition from a marine to a freshwater swamp was underway.

23

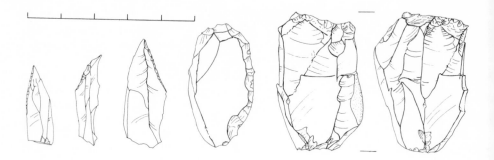

The presence of the first humans in the Levels is indicated by the discovery of hundreds of flint tools discarded on camp-sites on the islands in the Levels. Almost every sandy island, and some of the rocky islands, both north and south of the Poldens, were occupied by hunters and gatherers who must have moved about by logboat or raft across the expanses of open waters and reedy areas, and by foot over the hills and islands, in the quest for wild foods. These people hunted game, such as deer, wild pig and wild cattle, and many kinds of wildfowl. Fishing was another activity, as well as the gathering of wild plants which grew in abundance on the edges of the swamp and on the hill slopes. Equipment consisted of bow and arrow, throwing and stabbing spears, traps and snares, all made of wood and plant fibres; their flint arrowheads, knives and scraping tools are the only pieces to have survived.

The people were clad in the skins of the animals hunted and they had few possessions. Their campsites consisted of temporary windbreaks and shelters on the islands, where they would rest and plan their next movements through the Levels on a seasonal round of collecting and hunting. They disappear from our knowledge in the centuries before 4000 B.C., and we do not know how they reacted to the arrival of the first true settlers, except to suggest that they would probably have tried to avoid direct confrontation. There is some evidence to suggest that they moved to coastal areas in southern Britain, and concentrated their efforts on marine resources, but gradually they disappear from our record.

The Sweet Track

From 4500 B.C., farming communities became established in Britain, and developed a range of new activities. Their economy was one of mixed farming, growing cereal crops in forest clearings, keeping animals such as cattle, sheep and pigs and exploiting wild resources to a certain extent. Little is known of their domestic settlements, whether they lived in villages or isolated farms, and much of the archaeological evidence for the period comes from barrows and other impressive public monuments. Common among the surviving artifacts of the period are flint tools and stone axes, and pottery, and some of these items were widely exchanged across the country. By 4000 B.C., the new communities were well-established in several regions of Britain, including the Somerset Levels.

Their presence in the Levels is known through the discovery in 1970 of the oldest wooden structure yet found in the peat. Mr. Ray Sweet, a peat-cutter well known for his sharp eyes, was engaged in winter work clearing ditches, and he found low down in a ditch several solid worked timbers and, nearby, a flint arrowhead. He recognised the importance of these finds, and ensured that they were reported to the archaeologists. Preliminary work suggested that the timbers might come from a trackway, and the following summer the first stretch was excavated of what has since proved to be the earliest and perhaps the most important of the trackways in the Levels. It has been called the Sweet Track, after its discoverer.

The trackway was built across soft swamp-like ground where reeds and sedges grew, and there was often standing water. The aim of the builders was to provide a firm plank walkway raised above the water, and to do this they first laid long poles on the ground, end-to-end along the proposed route. These poles, or rails, were held in place by pegs, short pieces of wood sharpened at one end and driven obliquely into the ground like tent-pegs; the pegs were set in pairs or groups on either side of the rails, and together these two elements provided a firm substructure. Next, peat and vegetation was heaped up over the rails to give extra support to the planks that were then put in place, wedged between the groups of peg-tops, and lying parallel to the basal rails. In some places, a firmer base was needed and short lengths of spare planking, unused pegs and bits trimmed off the rails were wedged in between the main components to hold them firm. Finally, the ends of the planks were stabilised with slender vertical pegs driven through holes cut near the ends of the planks; these extended down into the peat, sometimes reaching the underlying clay.

Excavation at various points along the Sweet Track has shown that it was built along the line of an earlier structure, sometimes making use of its wood, and sometimes diverging from it by a metre or more. The earlier track, now known as the Post Track, consisted of hefty long planks placed on the marsh surface, and stout posts driven vertically into the ground at intervals of about 3m. Where the Sweet Track incorporated these posts they could have served as route-markers, but occasionally they were misleadingly to one side and may have lured the unwary traveller astray if the Sweet walkway was obscured by floodwaters.

The woods used to build the two structures differed slightly, and different species were used for different components. The majority of the posts have been identified as hazel, and the planks of the Post Track were split from ash and lime trees. The planks of the Sweet Track were made from oak-trees, each trunk being split into several pieces about 3-4m long and 60cm wide. The pegs, usually cut as short, straight lengths of branch about wrist-thickness, came predominantly from hazel and alder trees, with some elm, ash and holly being used too. The rails were from similar species.

The generally excellent state of preservation has made it possible to apply a wide range of studies to the wood from the Sweet and Post Tracks and most of our knowledge of Early Neolithic woodworking in Britain comes from these impressive structures. The people who built them 6000 years ago were undoubtedly excellent woodworkers. As we have seen, they seem to have deliberately chosen certain tree-species for certain functions, and they showed sound judgment in the way they exploited the properties of different woods. Oak splits readily and so was used for planks, and the trees were carefully selected to give strong straight timbers without knots and side-branches. Elm will also split, but is neither as straight nor as strong, and it was only rarely used to make planks. In the details of their woodworking, the skills of the craftsmen can also be seen, whether in shaping the end of a board to fit round some other piece, or sharpening a peg so that it would drive easily through the surface vegetation down into the peat below. All of this work was done with stone axes, knives and wooden wedges and mallets; Neolithic farmers had neither metal axes nor saws.

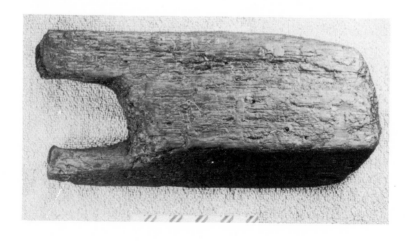

A variety of Neolithic artifacts has been found beside the Sweet Track, dropped by travellers or left by floodwaters, or deliberately hidden along the walkway. Amongst them was an unused flint axehead that had been acquired from a distant flintmine, perhaps near Salisbury, and a beautifully-made axehead of polished light green stone. This object was in perfect condition, as if it too had never been used. The stone has been identified as jadeite, a type of jade found sporadically on the continent.

Pottery, so common a find on settlement sites, is relatively sparse along the trackway. The broken pieces that have been found give the impression of pots dropped by accident by people walking along the narrow planks, and maybe slipping on a wet surface as they swung past one of the vertical posts. One group of sherds was associated with a concentration of hazelnuts, and was probably once a pot full of nuts, and another was found with a wooden stirrer or spurtle beside it, which may have fallen out when it was dropped. The pots are unusual, in that they all belong to the class of Neolithic fine-wares and there are no ordinary coarse domestic pots among them. Several were coated in a black clay slip and then burnished before firing, to give a shiny black surface.

A wooden dish was also found beside the Sweet Track, and it has since been conserved. It is a rare example of what was probably a fairly common Neolithic type.

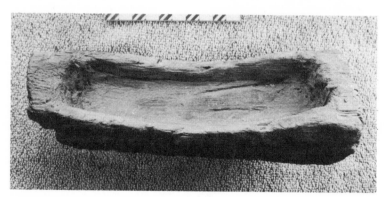

Neolithic people were hunters as well as farmers, and the marshy Levels provided a rich source of game for them. Several flint arrowheads have been found near the trackway, delicately flaked to make a strong, sharp tip shaped like a leaf, a form characteristic of the period. One of the arrowheads was found with a lump of sticky substance still adhering to its surface, and another retained a fragment of its split hazelwood shaft, bound with fine string made from nettle fibre. Many such arrowheads are known from elsewhere in the British Isles, but only very rarely do they retain any trace of shaft or binding.

The wooden pins associated with the track are unknown elsewhere, though a few bone objects of similar shape have been found. These pins were cut out of yew-wood, smoothed down and then bent into a bow-shape. Their function is not known, and suggestions include pins to make netting, pins to hold clothes in place, pins for the hair, or pins for decorating Neolithic noses.

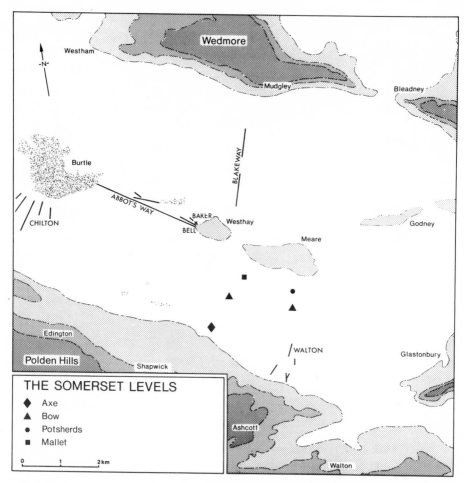

The Somerset Levels map showing locations including Westham, Wedmore, Mudgley, Bleadney, Burtle, Blakeway, Abbot's Way, Chilton, Baker, Bell, Westhay, Meare, Godney, Edington, Polden Hills, Shapwick, Walton, Glastonbury, Ashcott. Legend — THE SOMERSET LEVELS: ◆ Axe, ▲ Bow, ● Potsherds, ■ Mallet. Scale 0–2 km.

As the great reed swamp gradually shallowed through the buildup of peat, parts of the Levels became sufficiently dry and firm to support fenland trees such as birch and alder. These increased in extent until much of the area was covered by fen woodland, although the surface of the Levels was still wet, with pools of water, and winding streams where water flowed in from the hills around. The peat from this period, about 3500 B.C., is full of tree roots, drowned stems and branches, twigs and leaves, and also smaller marshland plants. The pollen record includes herbaceous plants suggesting an episode of clearance of the mixed oak forests on the islands and slopes, with more land being taken for agriculture and pasture. By 3000 B.C., an increase in water, mostly falling as rain, drowned the fen trees and initiated the growth of bog moss (*Sphagnum*), ling (*Calluna*) and cotton grass (*Eriophorum*).

Through this early period of raised bog formation, prehistoric man continued to occupy and utilise the variety of landscapes available to him, and we find abundant traces of his presence in the peats of 3500-2500 B.C. This is probably the first time that man occupied many parts of the Levels.

Two finds made by peat cutters are important. A mallet, made from the trunk and a branch of a yew tree, dates to 3000 B.C. Yew is a very heavy and hard wood, and its shaping into this mallet must have been a difficult task. The marks of bruising on both ends show where it had struck wooden pegs and posts, or wedges, in building houses and tracks, or splitting timbers. More spectacular is one half of a longbow, also of yew, which dates to 3500 B.C. The bow had broken at its grip, and when complete (as the drawing shows) it would have been 2 metres long, the first English longbow and antedating the mediaeval weapon by almost 5000 years. It is smoothed and bound with fat strips of hide and fine crisscross threads. Such a weapon might have cast an arrow 100 metres or more.

The Walton Heath hurdles

From 3500 B.C. onwards, prehistoric man built many wooden trackways across the marshland and fen woodland of the Levels. These linked the islands and the hills and they show a remarkable degree of organisation by the farmers and herdsmen in selecting routes, building and maintaining the trackways. Most of the paths are simple constructions, made of bundles of brushwood of birch and alder which were growing near at hand (p. 13). Several trackways, however, are more complex, and one of these is an outstanding discovery because it throws entirely new light on an activity about which we could otherwise know little.

The find was made on Walton Heath, when a peat machine scraped the surface of a wooden trackway which was soon reported and examined by archaeologists. The trackway was short, only 40 metres in length, and it consisted of a set of hurdles or panels laid down on a surface where open pools of water, wet hollows with moss, and slightly drier hummocks with heather created an uneven and rather treacherous route across the moor. Where this short trackway ended, the traveller could step onto a slightly firmer and drier natural surface requiring no building operation. Further south, a second stretch of hurdle trackway was found that continued the route from the Poldens across towards the Meare island.

34

The trackway on Walton Heath consisted of a large number of woven hurdles laid flat and slightly overlapping one another, to form a wide and immensely strong walking surface. Along the sides of the panels, pegs were driven in with a stout mallet so that the panels could not slip sideways. To prevent them sliding forwards or backwards, long poles were rammed into the body of each hurdle so that part of the pole rested on the adjacent panel. The effect must have been an immovable structure, although each panel would have been flexible enough to conform to the pressure of the loads passing over, and to the uneven bog surface beneath. In the central part of the trackway, a particularly difficult area was encountered, probably a deep pool of water, and the builders responded by dumping broken panels to form a foundation upon which they then laid the regular panels to form the walking surface. In places the trackway was five panels thick, and some tied double panels were used to give strength to the uppermost set. Due to extensive peat-cutting about 30 years ago, many of the panels were truncated as can clearly be seen in the photograph where the scale is positioned. Before the entire trackway was removed by modern peat-cutting, the Project lifted many of the panels and managed to preserve one of them completely; it is now in the County Museum, Taunton.

The Walton Heath hurdles were made in the traditional way, by selecting straight-grown shoots from coppiced hazel which was growing on the slopes and hills. The woodland consisted of many stools of hazel which had been cleared of their shoots at varying times, so that new shoots of varied ages and sizes were always available. For the hurdles, the craftsmen had gone through the woodland and had taken shoots of a uniform size (18-26mm in diameter), and of 3-9 years' age. This practice of selective clearing is called 'drawing', and because of the tree-ring studies we can state that the work took place during the summer months. Probably a stone axe was used to break the shoot from its stool, and this has been copied by experiment.

Each hurdle was made by selecting 4-6 shoots of slightly thicker character than the bulk, and setting them upright into the ground. Around these sails, as they are called, were then woven the thinner rods, each rod with an opposed weave to its neighbours, until the desired height (panel width) was achieved. The panels were large, 2-3 metres long and over one metre wide, and they each contained about 60 rods. At the edges, where the rods might slip out from the sail ends, the craftsmen used willow withies to tie the parts together. The result was a strong yet flexible panel, weighing about 30 kg (66 lbs), suitable for fencing and, on Walton Heath, for trackway building.

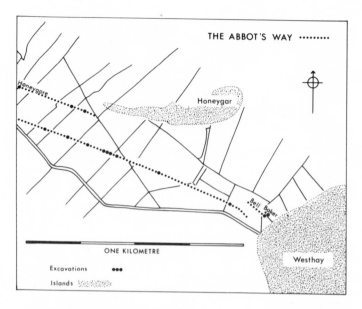

THE ABBOT'S WAY ·········

Honeygar

Honeygore

Bell Baker

ONE KILOMETRE

Excavations ●●●

Islands

Westhay

The growth of the great raised bogs in the centuries from 3000-2500 B.C. created a desolate landscape around the central island of Westhay-Meare. Settlement continued but at a reduced level, and many of the clearances were gradually lost to the encroaching forests. Nonetheless, the farmers and herdsmen retained some fields and pastures, and they continued to maintain communications by building trackways. Where the slopes of the raised bog met the island edges, in a 'lagg', run-off waters created difficulties of passage into and out of the marshlands. This problem was encountered at the western end of the island of Westhay, where a massive platform was built c. 3000 B.C. This structure, called the Baker Platform, lay just off the edge of the island. It was made by piling bundles and heaps of brushwood, supplemented by heavier stems and branches, onto the soggy ground so that a thick mattress was created. Joined to it were at least two trackways coming in from the bog, and a walkway linked the platform to dry land. For times of flood, a slipway descended from the platform for boats or rafts, and heavy mooring posts, worn by ropes, were held within the platform structure. In drier conditions, the trackways allowed people to cross the lagg onto the moor itself. The presence of dung beetles on the platform and the heavily worn nature of the trackways suggest that animals may have been driven across the structure.

Beneath one of the trackways was found a small carved figure of ash, only 15 cm (6″) high. It seems to represent a hermaphrodite, with both male and female aspects. It was placed head down (if we really think it had a head) and it might have been put there for some ceremonial purpose, or it might be only a casually whittled piece thrown away, or it might be a toy; it was christened 'god-dolly' by the archaeologists to cover some of the possibilities!

The Abbot's Way

The most famous wooden trackway in the Levels is a heavy structure running between Westhay and Burtle islands. This was first discovered in 1835 during peat-cutting on the Westhay Level. At Burtle, a priory had existed in mediaeval times, and at Westhay-Meare there were monastic buildings, of which the Abbot's Fishhouse now remains. The wooden structure, buried deep in the peat, was believed to be the connecting road and it was promptly named The Abbot's Way. We know it was built about 2500 B.C., too early for any abbot.

The roadway is wide and heavy, and it is a simple construction. The walking surface was made of split alder planks, with slats and branches filling the gaps. Along the sides of the roadway, long slender pegs were driven into the marsh to help hold the structure in place, and perhaps to mark the way when the walking surface was under flood waters.

The Abbot's Way was 2.5 km (1½ miles) long, and we can calculate the amount of timber required in its building. Over 30000 alder planks or split logs were needed, each about one metre long, and about 15000 pegs and stakes, of alder, hazel and ash. This must represent a considerable effort by the road-makers, in clearing woodland and preparing the components.

Environmental studies allow us to reconstruct the precise conditions of the marsh at this time. The roadway was placed directly on the treeless raised bog, which would have presented an uneven surface; the timbers ride up and down, and from side to side. Peat studies and beetle studies tell us that the bog consisted of a series of small stagnant pools of acid water, separated by tussocks and flatter patches of Sphagnum moss, cotton grass, heather and other plants. The builders would have tried to avoid the wettest parts of the bog, and the roadway curves around the pools.

Beside the timbers were found several small pellets of broken-up insects, representing the undigested remains of food, regurgitated from birds of the crow family. The largest pellet, 5 cm in diameter, contained the closely packed exoskeletons of over 250 beetles and fragments of about 200 ants; some of the beetles, and the ants, would not be living on the bog surface and must have been consumed in woodlands, and from anthills, on one or other of the islands nearby.

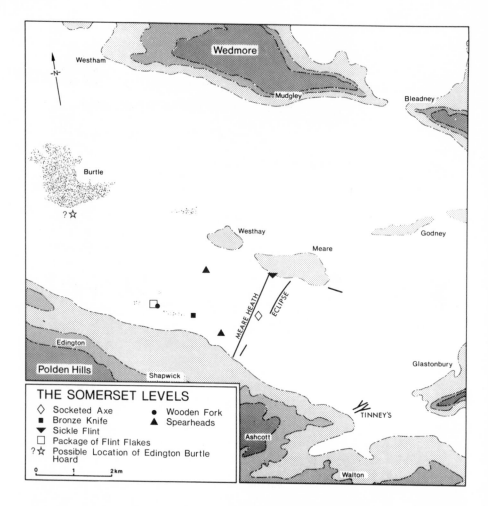

THE SOMERSET LEVELS

◇ Socketed Axe   ● Wooden Fork
■ Bronze Knife   ▲ Spearheads
▼ Sickle Flint
☐ Package of Flint Flakes
?☆ Possible Location of Edington Burtle
     Hoard

0   1   2 km

In the centuries after 2500 B.C., the great raised bogs of the Levels continued to develop, and to overwhelm and bury the successive attempts by man to build roadways, footpaths and platforms in the marsh. We do not know the rate at which the peat formed, but many structures probably lasted only a few years before being lost. The thickness of the peat in Shapwick Heath is said to have been as much as 10 metres (33 feet), and by the time the peat formation stopped, there was a sequence of prehistoric structures buried at differing depths in the peat. From 2500 B.C. to 1500 B.C. the attempts to maintain communications between settlements were sporadic, but thereafter there was a renewal of effort, which may represent the arrival of new groups of people who settled in various parts of the Levels.

One of the outstanding discoveries in the raised bog peats is the abundant evidence for prehistoric hurdles. We now know of several hurdle trackways of far greater length than the Walton Track. One is the Eclipse track, dated to about 1800 B.C., and forming a safe path across at least 1 000 metres of a wet marsh.

The panels used to make this track were 2 metres long and one metre wide, and they were made of coppiced hazel rods woven around long projecting sails. When this track was discovered, only a few centimetres of peat remained on top, and the panels were squashed by the recent passage of machines.

The Eclipse track helps to demonstrate the enduring presence of hurdle-manufacture in the Levels: in 3000 B.C. (Walton Heath), 2200 B.C. and 1800 B.C. (Meare Heath), 900 B.C. (Shapwick Heath) and 400 B.C. (Godney Moor); to this we can add the present-day craft of hurdle-making, and suggest that this represents the culmination of an industry which has existed for 5 000 years in Somerset.

There are several areas where prehistoric finds regularly appear as the peat is removed to lower and lower levels; one of these areas is Skinner's Wood, a small field beside three sand beds just north of the Polden Hills. High in the peats were a number of wooden trackways, Iron Age pottery and Bronze Age wooden objects including a hazel truncheon or handle or tenon (on p. 43). Lower down, in peats of 1600 B.C. a unique wooden tool was found; this is an implement of hazel carefully shaped for use as a hayfork or reedfork. Further down in the peats of 2200 B.C. another unusual find was made. Wrapped in layers of moss and cotton-grass were a number of flint flakes, unused and carefully packed for transport. Perhaps the small parcel fell from a traveller's sack, or from a boat during the season of floodwaters; whatever the reason, it came to rest in the marsh and was soon covered by the vegetation.

The Meare Heath Track

In the early 1930s, that indefatigable archaeologist Arthur Bulleid discovered a solidly-built wooden trackway in the peat cuts on Meare Heath. In the 1940s, the trackway was sighted again by Sir Harry Godwin at several points further south. In the 1970s, the track was again exposed by peat-cutting, and recorded in many places by the Project's Field Archaeologist. Along most of its length it was found to be badly damaged by peat-cutting and desiccation, but a few areas remained where excavation was worthwhile before the structure was finally lost.

By taking the evidence accumulated over the past 40 years, it is possible to reconstruct the Meare Heath Track. It was built over a fairly wet raised bog surface, at a time (1400 B.C.) when conditions may have been deteriorating. In places the surface was relatively firm thanks to matted vegetation of moss, heather and sedges. Elsewhere, the route crossed softer, wetter patches, and in these places

45

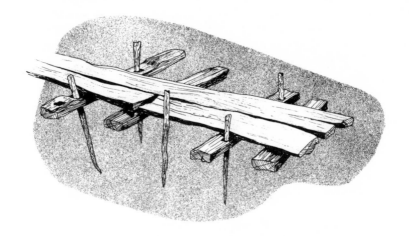

the first step in construction was to throw down quantities of small brushwood to fill the soft areas. This wood was cut from many different species of tree, including guelder rose and alder buckthorn as well as the more common hazel, alder and willow.

The walking surface of the Meare Heath Track was built almost entirely of oak timber, on principles similar to a railway line. At intervals, pairs of solid cross-beams were put down, in the manner of sleepers, making 'piers' every three metres or so. Parallel oak planks spanned the piers and provided the walking surface of the trackway. The crossbeams were held in place by long oak stakes, split out of tree-trunks and trimmed down with an axe. These stakes were driven through holes cut in the beams, and their projecting tops prevented the planks from slipping sideways.

Studies of the tree-ring patterns of the Meare Heath oak timbers have produced some interesting results. The trees from which the wood came were noticeably different to those used in the other planked walkway of the Levels, the Sweet Track. They were smaller, younger and less suitable for producing quantities of good planking, and were probably felled from secondary woodland in contrast to the primary forest exploited two thousand years earlier. It has proved possible to attribute some of the timbers to particular trees, due to the very close match of their ring patterns. This work has shown that a single tree might be split into planks, cross-beams and stakes, which were then scattered along several hundred metres of construction, mixed in with pieces from a number of other trees. This mixing suggests that the trees were processed where they were felled, on dry-land, and the components stock-piled until the trackway was built.

Near the northern terminal, at the base of the Meare Island, a single piece of flint was found during the excavations; it was a sickle blade, with an area of polish on one edge. It may have been used for cutting grasses, straw, reeds or possibly wood.

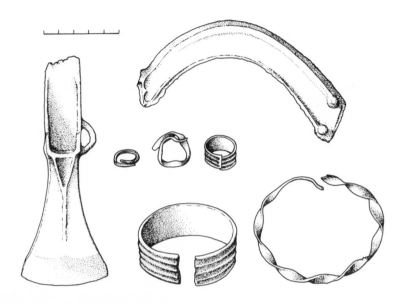

A wide range of later Bronze Age finds has been made in the Levels, including trackways, platforms, wooden tools, bronze implements, pottery and other objects. We know little about the trackways, because they were mostly cut away during the early years of commercial peat extraction. However, there are some objects that have survived. A century ago, a hoard of bronze tools and ornaments was found in a maple wood box buried in the peat near Edington Burtle. These objects date from about 1500 B.C. and must have been the possessions of a farmer, or possibly a merchant, who buried the box for safe-keeping but who never returned to claim it. Other finds more recently made include part of a necklace of amber beads, dropped in the marsh on Godney Moor; the amber originally came from Jutland and must have been a prized possession.

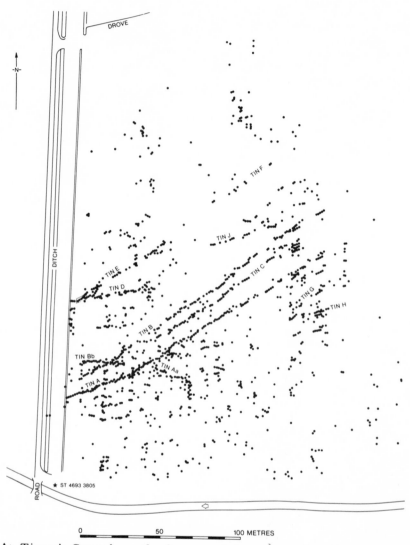

At *Tinney's Ground,* on the far east of the area we have been discussing, important discoveries were made by one of the Project's Field Archaeologists. During the first regular walking of newly-cut heads in this peat-field, a number of brushwood stems were noted, in the sections and in the cut mumps. The stems were grouped into bundles; some had cut ends (p. 50), and their presence was clearly the result of human activity. It was soon evident that the field contained a number of brushwood trackways, and for the rest of the 1970s it was the scene of frequent fieldwork and excavation.

48

Each time the field was cut, which might be two or three times a year, every head was walked to search for exposures of brushwood, and walked again to record each exposure and measure it in to a field plan, and again as each exposure was levelled. As cutting proceeded, new low heads were opened up, necessitating a new field plan. From start to finish of the fieldwork at Tinney's Ground almost every fixed point used in surveying was moved or disappeared: ditches were widened or filled, huts shifted, and the road-bridge with levelling mark demolished and replaced. Nevertheless, continuous surveillance of the field combined with excavation has made possible the reconstruction of the multiple trackways that traversed the bog-surface in this part of the Levels in 1400 B.C.

The construction of most of the tracks was very simple, consisting of bundles or armloads of brushwood placed longitudinally on the ground with their ends jammed together. One of the southern routes, Tinney's A (TIN A on the plan), was more complex. There were two distinct phases of construction, with a second track built directly over the first one. At one site on this route, a timber consolidation to the structure was found, with old oak planks and stakes underlying the brushwood; the upper layers of stems were carefully arranged, and strengthened at regular intervals by simple transverse branches. Another site, further east along the route, provided evidence of a junction, as the pathway split into two diverging lines. Immediately below this junction the earlier trackway was found to have done the same.

Pollen analyses and beetle studies have indicated that the dry land just south-west of Tinney's Ground, where the tracks lead, was used by farmers for growing crops and for pasturing animals. It is likely that the track-builders lived and worked here, on the Polden slopes, and built the tracks to venture out onto the bog for hunting and fowling expeditions, or perhaps to fish in the river Brue.

49

Many finds of the period 1000-500 B.C. have been made in the Levels. Among the wooden structures were several small hunting-blinds or shooting platforms, where the hunter with his bow and arrow could lie, concealed by reeds, awaiting the waterfowl. A dugout canoe from Shapwick may have helped retrieve the game, or transport reed bundles and other equipment across the floodwaters. Nearer the Poldens, the wet ground was consolidated in places by heaps of old planking from dismantled buildings. These planks, as well as the many sharpened branches and stems which helped to form the platforms and trackways, tell us much about Bronze Age woodworking techniques.

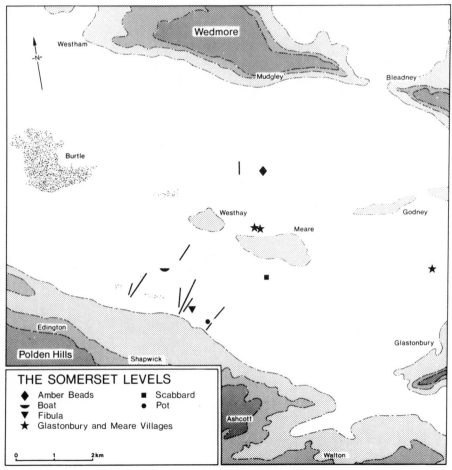

THE SOMERSET LEVELS

◆ Amber Beads   ■ Scabbard
➖ Boat   ● Pot
▼ Fibula
★ Glastonbury and Meare Villages

0   1   2 km

In the centuries from 1100 B.C., the Levels were subjected to periods of flooding from the Poldens and the Wedmore Ridge. This was mainly due to an episode of increased rainfall, and the peats of these flooding horizons are less humified and paler in colour than are the peats of slightly drier phases. Prehistoric farmers and hunters often built platforms and trackways during the flooding episodes, in order to maintain their traditional passages in the Levels, but even so there seems to have been a hiatus in major constructions in the centuries from about 700 B.C. to 400 B.C.; it is likely that the marshes were so wet that boat transport was easier to achieve than extensive trackway maintenance. About 400 B.C., perhaps a little earlier, two major settlements were established in the Levels, the first to be actually positioned in the marsh rather than on the edges. These two settlements are the famous 'Lake Villages' of Glastonbury and Meare.

51

The Glastonbury Lake Village

The settlement near Glastonbury was discovered in the 1890s by Arthur Bulleid, at the start of his lengthy involvement in local fieldwork. He had read of Swiss lakeside settlements and reasoning that the Somerset Levels provided similar conditions, he set out in 1888 on a deliberate search for remains. Four years later he discovered the site near Godney which soon became renowned as the Glastonbury Lake Village, and aroused considerable popular interest through the unusual variety of finds which it produced.

The Glastonbury site was excavated in the summer months for several years, funded by public donations, and directed by Bulleid and H. St. George Gray. Gray had worked with the most organised and productive archaeologist of the century, General Pitt-Rivers, and his training was put to good use at the new site. The area was methodically excavated and the finds recorded in considerable detail, and attention was paid to peat and plant remains, and food rubbish, as well as to more obviously exciting finds such as wooden tools, decorated bone and glass beads.

Environmental evidence shows that the settlement was built at some distance from dry land, out in the wilds of marsh and moor where the River Brue flowed sluggishly north. The settlement was probably close to a bend of the river for there was a landing stage on the eastern side of the village. There was no dry passage to the land mass dominated by Glastonbury Tor.

The village was surrounded by a wooden palisade, enclosing a heart-shaped area of about $3\frac{1}{2}$ acres. Inside, 89 mounds were found, formed by superimposed clay floors. Many of these had probably once been houses, and others were the floors of stables, workshops, cooking shelters or other domestic structures. The houses were round; most had a carefully-laid timber and brushwood foundation under the clay floor and some had a wooden floor over it. Walls were made of wattle and daub; the roof was probably thatched, with a good overhang to protect the walls from rain. Some houses had internal partitions, and they all had a carefully-built hearth, which was often remodelled over the years.

The plan of the site suggests there were 5-7 groups of houses and huts, with paths and open spaces between them; this grouping may reflect the social composition of the community which could have consisted of 5-7 family groups, forming a population of around 100 people.

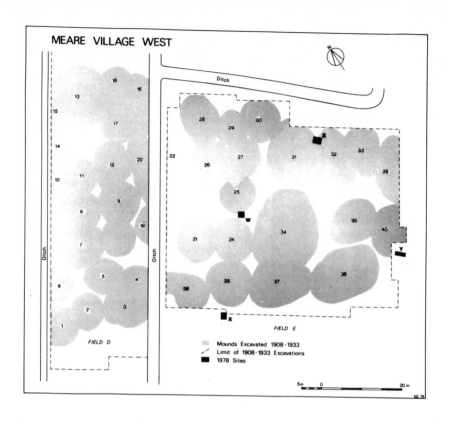

MEARE VILLAGE WEST

Ditch

FIELD D

FIELD E

Mounds Excavated 1908-1933
Limit of 1908-1933 Excavations
1978 Sites

5m   0   20 m

The Meare Lake Village

The settlement at Meare was also found by Arthur Bulleid, in 1895. The excavations of the Glastonbury site were in progress, and a local farmer who had seen the finds brought in a small parcel of similar objects from one of his fields. When Bulleid went to the find spot, he came across mounds similar to those at Glastonbury, and pottery in the face of the field-ditch. The investigation of the Meare site began in 1908, the year following the last of the Glastonbury excavations.

Two separate groups of mounds were identified, now known as Meare Village West and Meare Village East. Bulleid and Gray excavated at both sites over a period of many years, and they investigated the intervening ground, searching for a causeway linking the villages. Such a link was never found, but they did come across several heaps of cereal-grain instead. In the mid-1960s, excavations resumed under the direction of Michael Avery of Queen's University, Belfast, and then for 10 years no further work was carried out.

Early in 1978, the Somerset Levels Project made a trial investigation at the eastern end of Meare Village West, which picked up traces of the previous excavations, and produced samples for peat and pollen analysis, tree-ring and beetle studies, and radiocarbon dating. The results showed that enough evidence remained for these recently-developed techniques to be profitably applied to the site. Since it was also clear that the water-table had fallen in recent years, the Project obtained permission to excavate the western end of the western village before valuable evidence was lost through the drying ground conditions. The bountiful and varied evidence from this recent work, together with the evidence from previous sites, makes it possible to put together some picture of the original settlement.

The immediate environment was dominated by raised bog, where an impoverished vegetation of heather, sedge and moss grew on a surface dotted with shallow puddles of stagnant rainwater. Typically, raised bogs grow in a domed formation (see p. 5), and so the surface probably sloped gently upwards away from the settlement to the north. One hundred metres to the south was the lias island of Meare, dry, forested, and ideal for cultivation or pasture. Between the settlement and the island was a lagg, a low wet area fed by water draining from the island and from the raised bog. There may even have been a stream flowing to the west, with alder and willow trees growing along its banks.

The settlement itself was undoubtedly different from Glastonbury. There was no palisade, and apparently no need for substantial foundations, and there may not have been any permanent dwellings.

The inhabitants of Glastonbury and Meare were farmers, keeping animals, growing crops and using the wild resources that were available in plenty around them. There is evidence from both sites for sheep as the most common domestic animal, with cattle and pig in fair numbers, some horses, and dogs which probably helped in herding the flocks.

Sheep provided meat, and perhaps milk, and were certainly kept for their wool. The frequency of spindle whorls suggests the production of yarn was common-place, and there is also evidence for weaving. Cattle would have been kept for milk and meat. Evidence for the latter is available in the quantity of butchered, fragmented and burnt bones. Milk is not directly obvious, but some of the variety of wooden tubs and pails may have been used in milking and cheese-making. Cattle also provided skins for leather, and horn for tools, and some oxen were kept for their strength, to pull ploughs or carts and waggons.

The evidence for arable farming is varied: pollen from weeds that grow in arable fields, carbonised seeds in plenty, and equipment for gathering and processing the harvest. Wheat, barley and rye were grown, harvested with sickles and probably stored in pots or baskets. Some of the grain was ground into flour using a saddle quern, and rotary querns were also in use. Another crop was a small bean, not unlike a broad-bean or field bean. The crops cannot have been grown on the raised bog; for Glastonbury, the nearest suitable ground was on the Godney island or the dry land of the present-day settlement. For Meare, the fields

were probably much closer, on the dry lands of the lias island just across the lagg, and Bulleid noted that far more grain was found at Meare than at Glastonbury.

Food and raw materials also came from the moors, marshes and forests of the vicinity. Many bones of wild birds have been identified, especially migratory water-fowl and several species of duck which could have been present all year. The pelican-bones from Glastonbury, and other now rare species such as the black grouse show that many more favourable and extensive habitats were available for birds then than now. Surprisingly few fish-bones have been found, despite sieving of the occupation deposits. Wild animals such as deer and boar were occasionally hunted, and several smaller species were probably taken for their fur, notably otter.

Many wild fruits such as elder, sloe, apple and blackberry were eaten, and plants were doubtless collected for medicine and for dyes. Reeds were available for thatching, and reeds or withies could be used to make baskets, whilst stouter hazel and oak were chosen for hurdles.

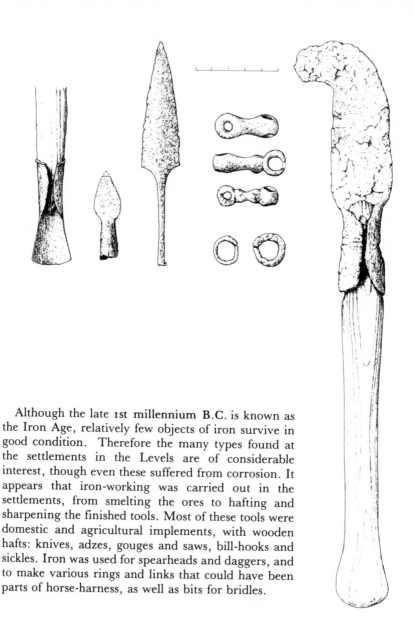

Although the late 1st millennium B.C. is known as the Iron Age, relatively few objects of iron survive in good condition. Therefore the many types found at the settlements in the Levels are of considerable interest, though even these suffered from corrosion. It appears that iron-working was carried out in the settlements, from smelting the ores to hafting and sharpening the finished tools. Most of these tools were domestic and agricultural implements, with wooden hafts: knives, adzes, gouges and saws, bill-hooks and sickles. Iron was used for spearheads and daggers, and to make various rings and links that could have been parts of horse-harness, as well as bits for bridles.

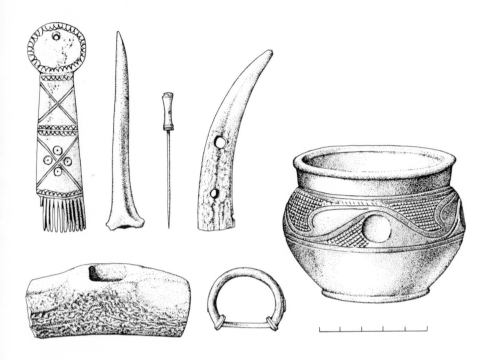

Many objects and tools were made of materials other than iron. Flint was still in use at Meare, and several types of local stone were used as querns, grinders, polishers and hammer-stones. Bone, horn and antler were made into weaving combs, awls and needles, polishers, hammer-heads, little boxes, spindle whorls, handles for knives and other tools, cheek-pieces for bridles, rings, and other objects whose use we can only surmise. Lead and tin were occasionally used for fishing weights or spindle whorls, and bronze was relatively common for tweezers, needles and other delicate objects. Clay was used for crucibles and spindle whorls, and especially for pottery which was produced in a wide range of fabrics and styles, and sometimes highly decorated. Some patterns were used on diverse fabrics and objects, such as the dot and circle motif applied to clay pots, wooden tubs and bone boxes or weaving combs. Splendid Celtic curvilinear designs were executed on pots of a type known as Glastonbury ware, and carved also on wooden containers.

Wood was more commonly preserved at Glastonbury than at Meare and most of our knowledge comes from the excavations at the turn of the century. It is clear that wood was a vital raw material, for building and fencing, for large items such as boats and waggons, and for making a host of everyday objects. Handles for metal tools have survived, and tools that were made entirely of wood, such as mallets. Wooden tubs were made, some of them decorated in the same way as the pottery, and many fragments of dishes and spoons or ladles were found, along with bungs or stoppers and other small domestic objects. The function of certain pieces of worked wood is not always clear, but some appear to be components for a loom, and others for composite wooden wheels with spokes.

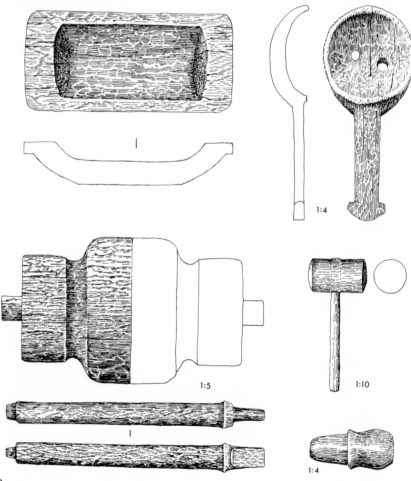

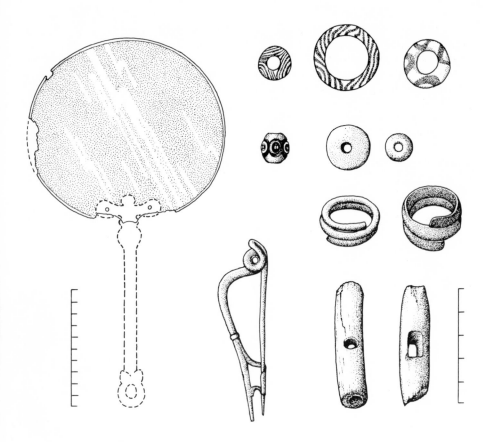

The inhabitants of the Levels may have been quite strikingly dressed, judging by the variety of ornaments that has been found. Beads of amber, glass and shale were either strung as necklaces and bracelets, or sewn onto clothing. The glass beads may have been manufactured in the settlements, and were produced in several shapes and sizes in vivid blues and yellows, and as beads with a patterned spiral. Shale bracelets were made, both plain and decorated. Toggles or clothes-fasteners were carved out of bone and antler, and sometimes decorated with typical dot and circle motifs. Bronze was used for rings and brooches, and for a polished mirror to admire the full effect of all this finery. (In the illustration the mirror is shown half-size compared to the other objects).

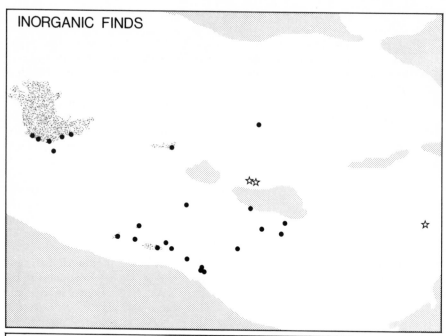

INORGANIC FINDS

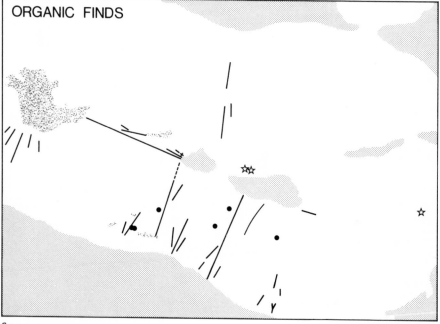

ORGANIC FINDS

With the abandonment of the settlements at Glastonbury and Meare, almost certainly due to declining environmental conditions, the evidence for prehistoric occupation of the Levels comes to an abrupt end. Several centuries later, in 250 A.D., a great transgression from the sea brought marine waters and silts and clays onto the western margins of the raised bog, and into the northern part of Godney Moor. By 400 A.D. the bogs were in effect dead, with growth stopped due to a reduction in the annual rainfall needed to maintain their development.

During the cutting of the upper peats, several hoards of Roman coins and other objects have been found; these had been deliberately buried, probably for safe-keeping. Otherwise, there is no trace of any substantial interest in the marshlands from the abandonment of the Iron Age villages until the time of the written records of monastic activities.

With these histories we come to the end of the prehistoric past and begin the story of man's endeavours to drain the Levels. Without the peats, our prehistoric records would be sparse indeed; without waterlogging, we would have only the inorganic finds of stone, flint and pottery, and the map (at top) would be sadly incomplete. In contrast, the finds of wood and other organic substances provide a much clearer picture of the extent of human activity in the prehistoric past, and through our archaeological and environmental studies, we can now point to the importance that the Levels had for prehistoric man. Hills, slopes, islands and marsh all combined to offer a great range of potential materials, if man was only adaptable enough to take advantage of them. The archaeological record preserved in the peat shows that man did indeed seize his opportunities. Hunting and gathering of wild resources in the forests and in the marshes combined with cereal production, cattle rearing and woodland activities, to yield a variety of supplies well capable of supporting prehistoric communities around the Levels.

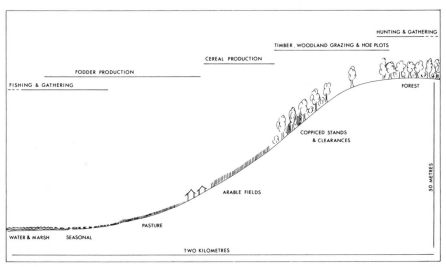

THE FUTURE

The unique character of the Somerset Levels is based on water. Waterlogged to a great extent for 6000 years, the Levels still flood today when the winter rains choke the river systems. Waterlogging created the peatbogs which contain, or contained, a unique record of man and environment.

The peatlands began to be removed at least 800 years ago, and cutting and draining have continued to exert their toll ever since. In areas where peat-cutting has been extensive, archaeological finds have also been great, and if cutting continues and is extended into new areas, then archaeology too will continue to yield new evidence about the first human settlers. The co-operation of the peat companies in archaeological work has always been generous. Of far greater seriousness for archaeology today is the question of water-levels and drainage. As the peats are drained and dry out, the organic evidence contained within them also dries out and rapidly decays beyond recognition. The effects of modern drainage can be seen today in the partial decay of the oldest roadway in the world, the Sweet Track (p. 25), and in the disintegration of the relics from the latest settlement at Meare (p. 54). These two sites, and all those between them in age, in fact the entire prehistoric record, had been intact for over two thousand years until today's drainage operations began their irreversible destruction.

Only if archaeologically significant parts of the Levels can now be preserved, and other parts offered for commercial work, will archaeology be able to continue its attempts to retrieve, analyse, understand and conserve those aspects of our prehistoric past which cannot be found anywhere else in this country.